Edition Schott

Piano · Klavier

Nikolai Kapustin

Николай Капустин

* 1937

Capriccio

(1992)

for Piano
für Klavier
для фортепиано

opus 71

Authorized Edition

ED 23155
ISMN 979-0-001-20785-0

www.schott-music.com

SCHOTT

Mainz · London · Madrid · Paris · New York · Tokyo · Beijing
© 2019 Schott Music GmbH & Co. KG, Mainz · Printed in Germany

Capriccio

opus 71

Nikolai Kapustin
*1937

4

rubato romantico

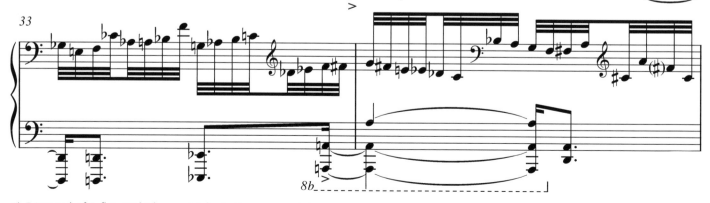

*) E instead of E-flat might be a mistake in the manuscript.

stringendo

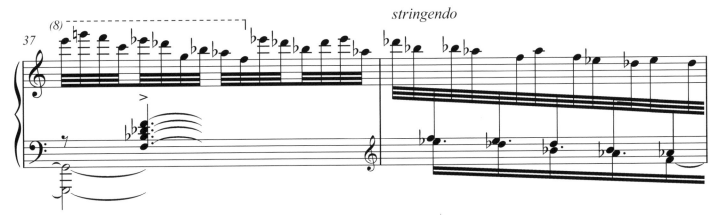

Moderato (♩ = 120)

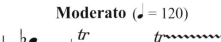

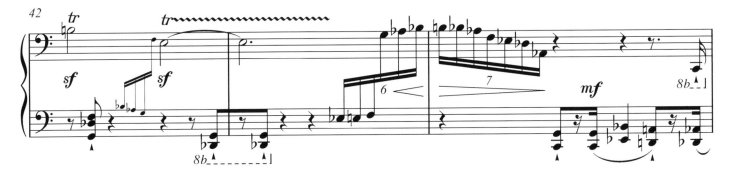

with a relaxed beat

poco rit.　　a piacere

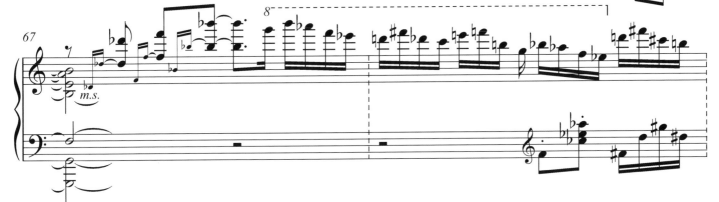

Allegro assai (♩ = 138)

8

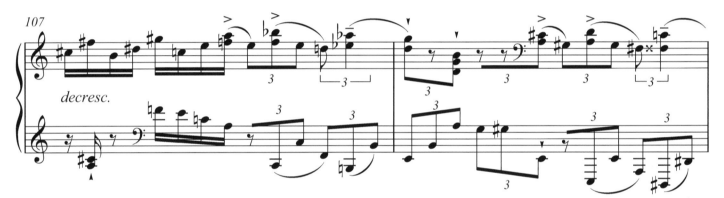

Largo (♩ = 51)

♪ = ♩ *scherzando*

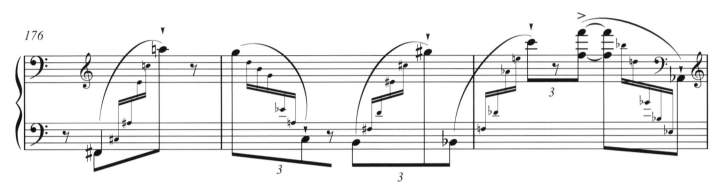

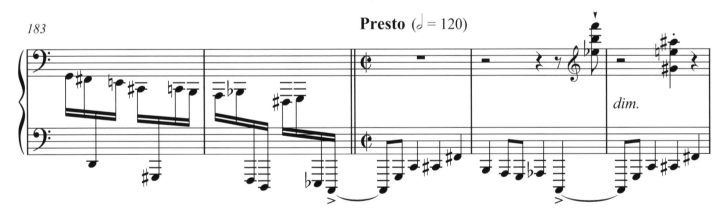

Presto (♩ = 120)

dim.

mp

192

196

200

204

rinf   mf

208

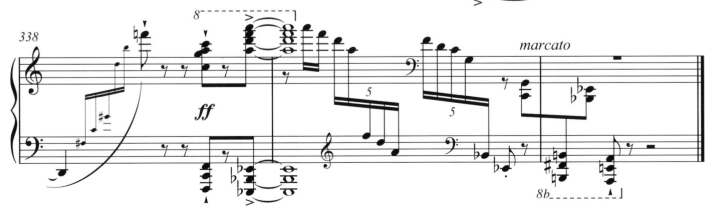